Tim and the Computer

A computer training storybook for Toddlers – ages 2 to 4 years.

by
Dennis E. Adonis

Illustrations by:
Darko Ristevski

Published by:
Learning Tree Media

Tim and the Computer

Learning Tree Publishers
West Sussex
Great Britain

Ordering Information:
For distribution details, please contact the publisher at:
learningtree.uk@gmail.com
www.learningtree.tk

First Printing, June 2012

An open letter to Parents

Dear Parents,

You would acknowledge that children are much smarter and technologically adapted than us when we would have been there age not so long ago.

Kids are almost overnight experts at reprogramming our smartphones, the game box and most computerize gadgets than even their parents, most of the times.

Until a few years ago a book of this nature would have been inconceivable, since most parents would have thought that teaching a 2, 3 or 4 year old the fundamental aspects of computers, as practically unnecessary for a child of that age.

Ironically, today we have no other choice but to accept that a child without computer knowledge, even as small as a toddler, can encounter serious difficulties to adapt to a computerize school environment later on, and by extension, find it difficult reason effectively on such topics with children of his/ her age.

It is almost every good parent wish that there child receives nothing but the best that life has to offer, and in essence, the best education.

And your desire to give them the best education in computers rests deeply in the pages of this book.

This book forms the foundation of a series of children literature focused on helping kids to better understand the fundamental aspects of computers.

Children at the age of 2 to 4 (and even beyond) are more inclined to learn from stories rather than a direct instructional method.

It would be sheer boredom and difficulty to get a child to effectively learn about computers unless there is a consistent, well put together story that actually teaches the child under the guise of telling them a tale. It is by far the best way by which the child would have an interest in what is being taught.

Storybooks makes kids interested in the subject being taught, and provide a more simplified way in which recollection of the subject matter can be achieved.

It is via this method that respected Educational Author, Dennis E. Adonis seeks to help children better understand and retain essential aspects of a computer system, and by extension, help them to use it more effectively.

After all, you can better use something if you understand what it is about, how it works and its many purposes.

Therefore, your decision to get your child a copy of this book was certainly an excellent choice, and open evidence that you care about their academic development and future survival in a technologically advancing generation.

Learning Tree Publishing

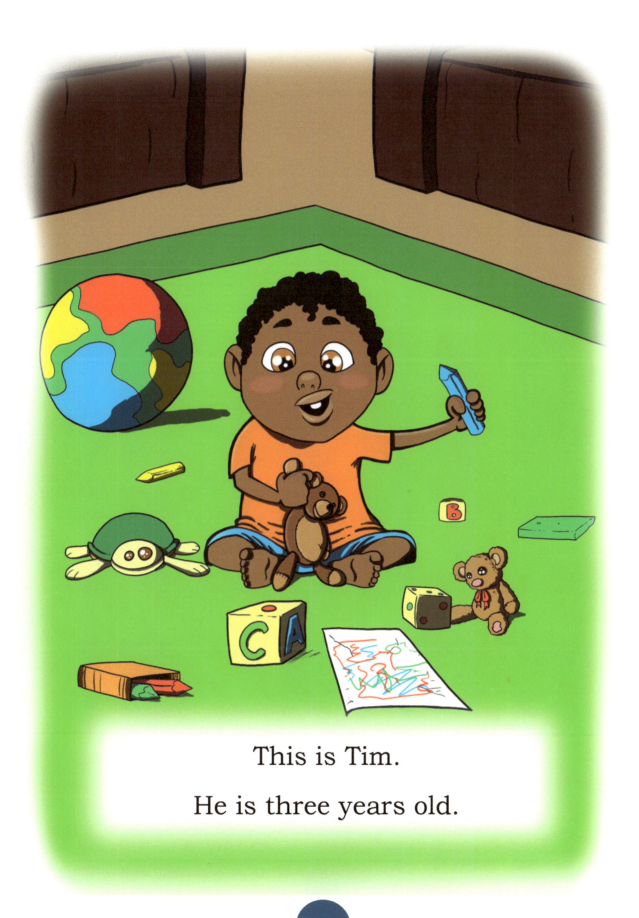

This is Tim.

He is three years old.

There is a computer in Tim's home.

It is called a <u>Desktop Computer</u>.

Tim loves to use the computer.

He loves its big shiny screen too.

The screen is a part of the computer.

The computer has many other parts.

Tim asked the computer ......

Why it has so many parts.

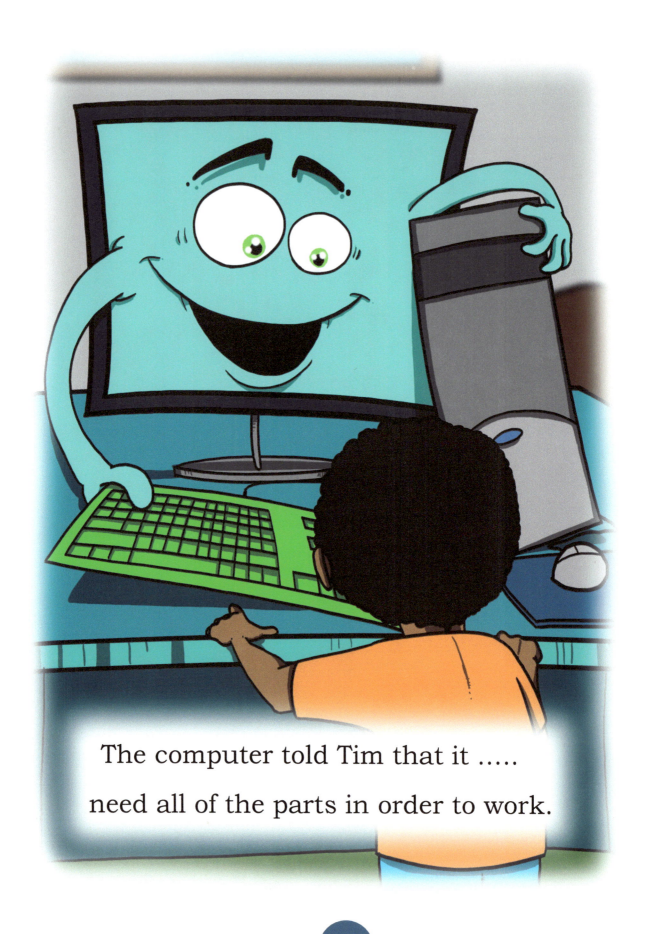

The computer told Tim that it .....
need all of the parts in order to work.

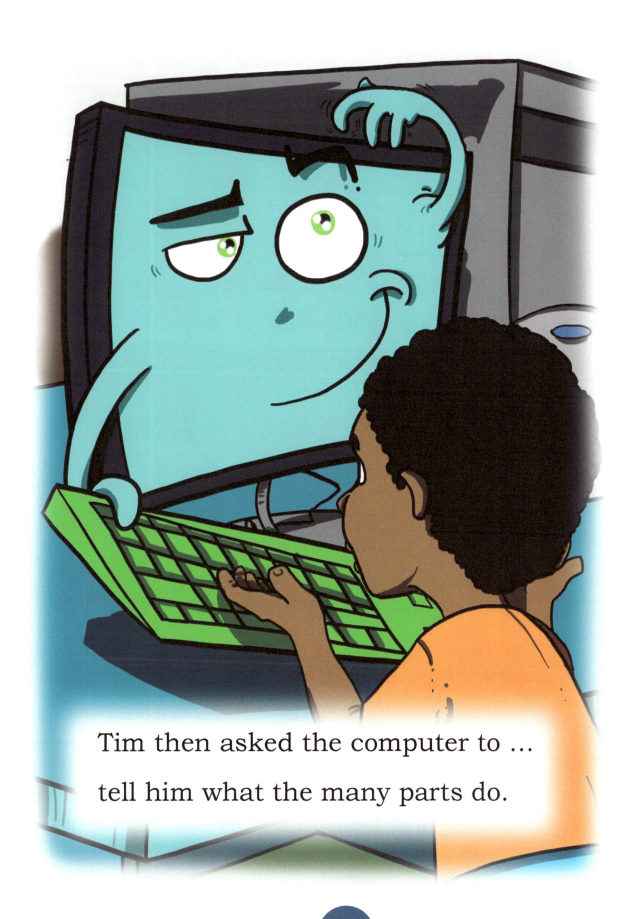

Tim then asked the computer to ... tell him what the many parts do.

The computer smiled and said ...

... "ok Tim, I will tell you".

"I use this screen to show you pictures and other things", it said.

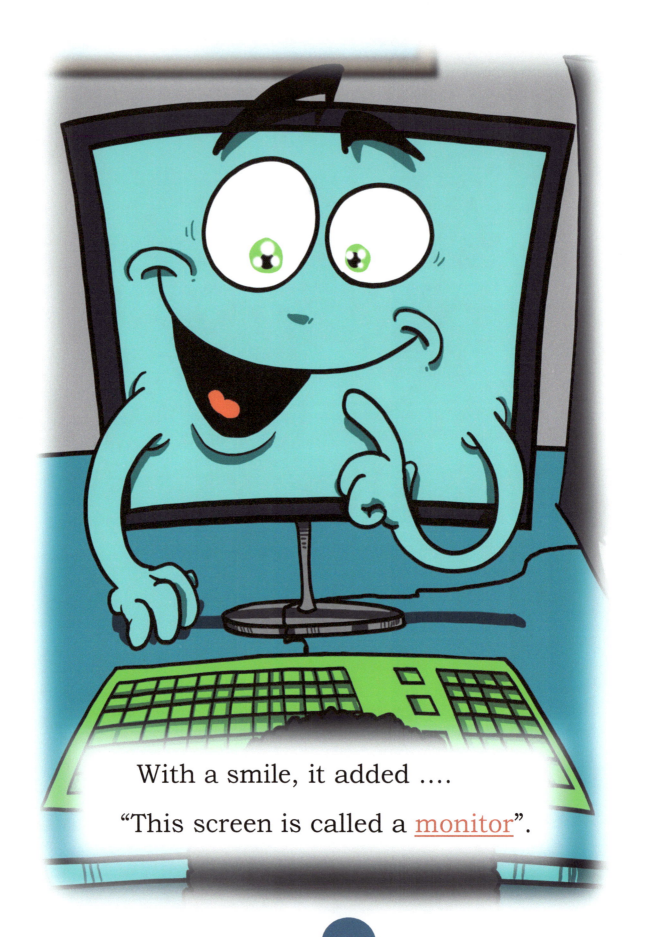

With a smile, it added ....

"This screen is called a <u>monitor</u>".

"The monitor shows things that are ... in my brain or things you want to see".

"Pictures, words, and other things …

.... are usually stored in my brain".

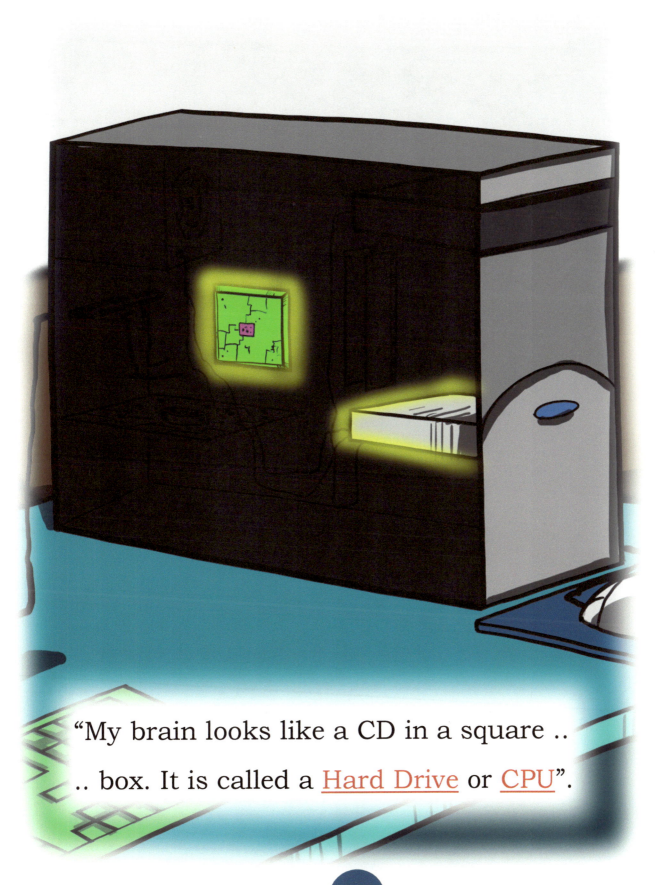

"My brain looks like a CD in a square ...

... box. It is called a <u>Hard Drive</u> or <u>CPU</u>".

"My brain stores lots of stuff", he said.

"It is hidden away inside a CPU <u>Tower</u>".

"A keyboard is plugged into the tower ..
to types things that you see on screen".

"A <u>mouse</u> is plugged in to move, point …

… and click on things on the monitor".

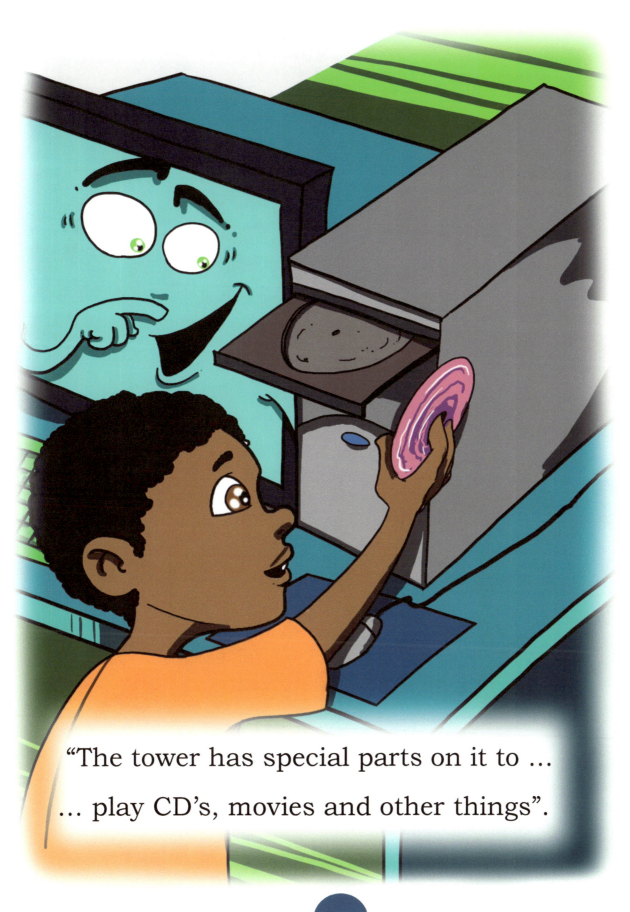

"The tower has special parts on it to ...

... play CD's, movies and other things".

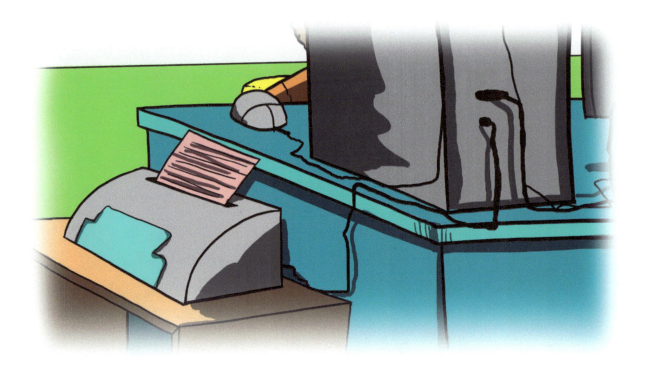

"It also has special holes to plug in ...

... the speaker, printer, and more".

"My brain controls all things that ...

... are plugged into the <u>tower</u> unit".

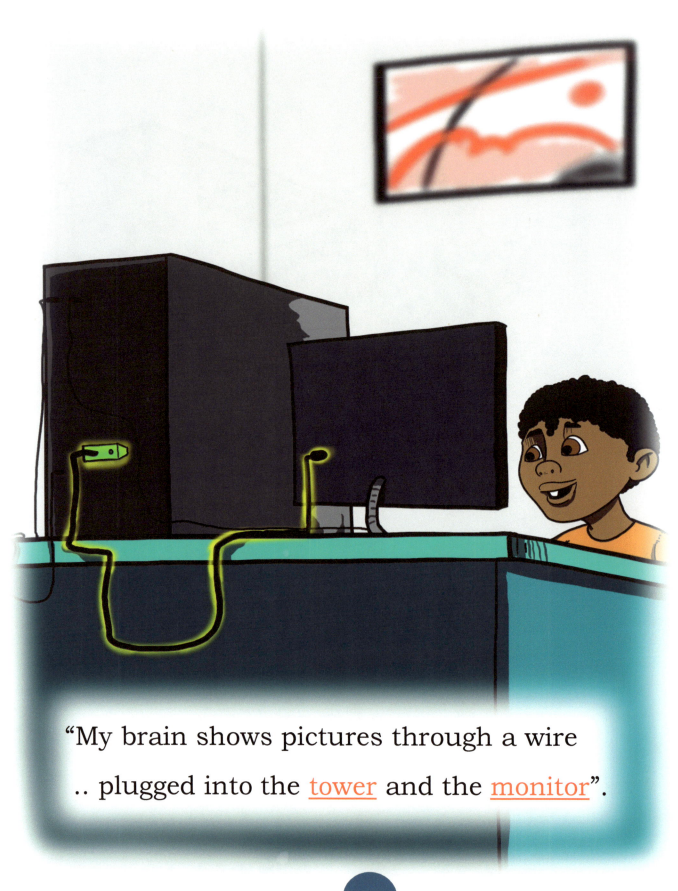

"My brain shows pictures through a wire
.. plugged into the <u>tower</u> and the <u>monitor</u>".

"Pictures from my brain and the net ....

.. goes through the wire to the monitor".

"To turn me, press this button on the tower ..

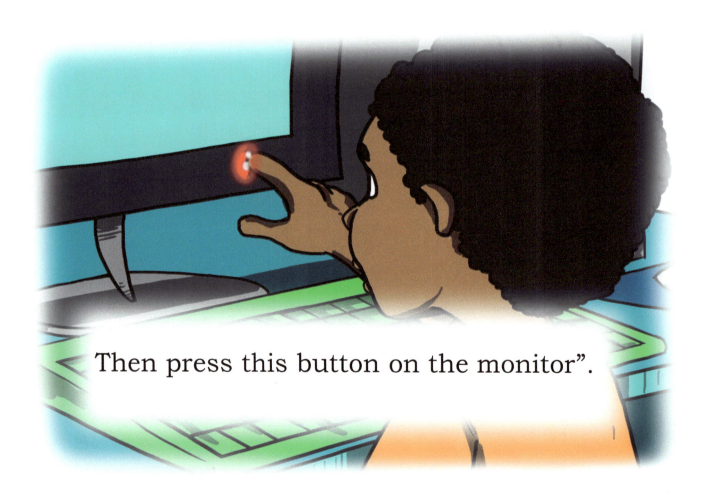

Then press this button on the monitor".

"My screen will light-up when I am on.
You can then use me to do many things".

"There are many types of computers.

They may also have different shapes".

"But we almost do the same things ....

.. because we are all called computers".

Tim was happy that the computer ....
.. had told him so much about itself.

He then called over his mom and told ..

.. her what he learnt about computers.

Tim's mom was happy that he had ....

.. learnt so much about computers.

She then turn to the tired computer …

.. and click on the word "<u>shut down</u>".

The computer then began to sleep ....

.. while Tim went off to bed, happily".

The End

About the Author

Dennis E. Adonis is a prominent Guyanese Computer Software Engineer, Musician, Educational Author and Folk Novelist.

As of May 2012, he had written over a dozen books, half of which are based on Computer Science, including four children books in the same spirit as this one.

Mr. Adonis, himself a father of five adorable children, is known to be an excellent mentor and educator as it relates to helping children to understand the fundamental aspects of Information Technology regardless of their age grouping.

He had served as a mentor on many Children's computer teaching projects in the Caribbean and Europe, and had headed two *Unicef* assisted-projects aimed at teaching computers to children in his home country Guyana between 2005 and 2006.

His educational background in a variety of fields has also allowed him to be avail as a consultant for various entities over the years, but mostly as a Computer Security Software Engineer.

Outside of his work as an outstanding Author, he is currently a Contributing writer on Information Technology at Yahoo.com, and an *Adjunct* Curriculum Developer in Information Technology at Warnborough College, in England.

To interact with the Author, visit his Official Website at: **www.dennisadonis.net**

Author's Bio compiled by: Ms. Deon Brown
Learning Tree Publishing – Great Britain.